T0328507

Renegade

Femi Morgan

Published in Nigeria by The Baron's Café
An imprint of Fairchild Media

Plot 1-4, Adewumi Layout, Akinyemi, Ibadan
media@fairchildmedia.com.ng
www.fairchildmedia.com.ng
+2348068108018

ISBN: 978-978-959-329-3

Cover design: Innocent Ekejuiba
Book Design: Oluwasogo Moses Faloye

Praise for Renegade

In this collection of poems, Renegade, Femi Morgan's unconventional images and diction bring freshness to a variety of themes, including love. The familiar and unfamiliar, the sacred and the secular, far and near, and old and new come together in unexpected circumstances that defy expectation in flowing lines that sharpen the appetite to read on and on. In many ways, these are "renegade" poems as far as the tradition of modern Nigerian poetry is concerned. The outlaw persona of the poet brings vitality to the poems. Pros and newcomers to poetry will find reading these poems a fulfilling experience.

Tanure Ojaide, a poet and scholar.
Frank Porter Graham Professor of Africana Studies,
University of North Carolina at Charlotte, USA.

With clever, striking imagery, 'Femi Morgan offers a mordant portrayal of modern life

Adebiyi Olusolape
Critic and Poetry editor, Saraba Magazine

Femi Morgan's "Renegade" is a rich collection of poems that are provocative and clever. Dealing with a wide range of topics—including love, life, death, God, and politics—Morgan delivers surprising morsels of imagery and symbolism. He uses words, metaphors and phrasing that paints pictures of realism and fantasy. His references swing widely from the local to the global, from Sango to Skype, and from bitter leaf soup to Oprah.

Femi Morgan is delightfully irreverent, offering a lyrical palette that amuses, teases, and inspires. In "Eye", Morgan explains that "poets are the strings that hold God's heart." That phrase exemplifies this collection beautifully and captures the poet implicitly.

Stephanie Shonekan, PhD
Chair, Department of Black Studies,
University of Missouri, Columbia, USA

The song of a bard in step with the masters. Renegade is delightful.

Efe Paul Azino
Performance Poet & Director, Lagos International Poetry Festival, Nigeria

Femi Morgan's 'Renegade' is a beautiful bouquet of poems written with an inspirational young energy. He chooses his themes wisely and treats them with knowledge and insight. Humour and deep seriousness balancing on a tight rope. The voice is trustworthy and genuine.

Niels Hav
Writer & Danish Poet Laurete
Winner of the Danish Arts Council Award and Author of We are Here,

A journey uninhibited! A call to self expression!

Silva Imal
Visual Arts Curator and founder, Imal Art Consortium

To my father, Chief Sunday 'esike Morgan who said 'you should write another book'

Selected Poems

Bar Room Conversations

Postcards for Irene

New-Inverse

Two Legs

Author's Note

About The Author.

Selected Poems

German Machines

Men are from Mars
Women are from bitterleaf soup
Flowers are made from plastic
Recycled from nearby dump sites
Shit and all

Men are from Earth
Don't let anyone lie to you
They are just dust
Even when the eyes tickle you
And the muscles are six feet tall

Women are from ...
Rumour has it
That they are produced by
A chromosome making lab in Germany
Delicate, beautiful and 'soft-hearted'

Fly like a Bird
(In memory of Aramide)

Fly like a bird
No one can hold you
Float on the chariot of shouts
and tears
that wail your name
Hear not the din of broken china
Fly like a bird.

A Good Poet

A poet dies with a toothpick of verse
In his mouth
The poet will not bow to death
Cover cloths of death

A good poet
Cannot hate, else he won't write good poetry
But love and anger are allowed
Negritude and Apartheid poems are allowed

Rhythm without sense
Words without common sense
Rhyme without real dreams...

Silence is allowed

A good poet
Must steer clear of the gospeller's gossip
For lampoon is allowed
Mini-skirting imagery is allowed
Feminist agenda is allowed

When poem mocks without language
When it builds without fencing..

Silence is allowed

Silence is allowed
Like the missing imam on Friday noon
Silence is a missing linesman
A pothole admits its presence
A tender mouth sucks protesting breasts

Silence is allowed

A couple of tribalist cows
The tightrope tightens like an action-packed condom
Condominium
Love in Tokyo
Wakes in Nigeria
Super Egg rolls
God fore-bid in a one chance

Silence

Time Flies

Time flies
my mother likes to fry garden egg
forthe new yam
Sh plucked it from her backyard
sanctuary
where she sang her own Negro spiritual.
The song tasted on my tongue when it
glided on my lips.
Now I live in a concrete jungle
where all that grows are facades of weed
Sprouting, forcing themselves to grace
the sun.

Time flies
I choose my memories
The ones that keep me awake
The sizzling dodo pestered by tomato
sauce
Scrambled eggs
Joustled for by my folks from Illinois
Plantain was cheap and we could afford it
we were rich as long as we were not
men of NADECO
the military left us alone by being jailed
but there was food
Now I live in this concrete jungle
Bursting forth from cracked dinosaurs

My backyard filled with rhetorics and
empty stomachs
Only double speak eats and gets married
Truth goes hungry to work and to bed.

Time flies
I want to go back to childhood when I
read newspapers to please my father
Now it is used for balls of Akara
The hustle is in print
The words painted like a collage that
nobody reads
Reddened by the blood of men with voices
but it was sweet.

Food is like a present
the leaves we wrap them are the
breasts of hope
But in this concert jungle
Food is fixed into tunnels of cardboards
Thrown into recycled nylon
Foisted on us by the Go-slow to work
Our lives and balanced diet is a farce
Our food is the fertiliser of the politician
The aromatic weed that puts us line
Fura, Wara, Obi Abata, Kuli kuli, Abacha
Dodo Ikire, Kpukpuru, all waging the wars
of modernity, distance and pocket infrastructure.
Minimum wage for coke.

Time flies
There is no way to end this tale
As memories linger like tears in my eyes
They shut the doors and open them to the aroma
of my mother's cooking
The risky burgers of my adulthood
so when I travel to the embrace of mama
She weeps for what the city has made me

Time flies

I do not belong to you

So cold is my lot
And those happenstances
Of warmth
Is a war fronting at my being

I am not carved for fame
I have only dreamt of a peaceful fortune
But my tongue has tarred my progress
My song has quickened my mortar
No bodies strewn on my path

I am not a poet
I am not a writer
I am an imposition
Spoken word swag
Dreadlocks
 prevent me
From the mirror
My profile in frantic search
For shelter amongst bowlegged cunts

Fuck

I will not write

You in a song
time will pass
And new songs will drown
The waves of our joy

I will not write
For you
Because I cannot retract
My words
When it all falls to the ground
Germinating the pain
Reminders of folly

I will not etch
Your name in the deep smitchens*
Of my heart
The larger, blown up in civil wars
Leaving words amputated
You remind me of the shape
Of death I once died
Cremated to the bones
The wails of cold blood, burning in my veins

*Smitchens is a self-created compound derived from snitch
and smidgen

Diffidence

I will not join words
with you
I will join words without you
with hyphenated angst
I will string them into colossi manifest

Today may be the worst day
but when it is past 12, it is another
fresh with its own "Joke of the Day"

I will not join words with-
the name of animal, place and things
I will bask in the alpha-numerals
mind blowing decimals that defecate everywhere
like goats in Okonkwo's compound

I will not join words with you
I am not a tailor
cutting and pasting in references
like Google Search

I will laugh like frequent "go-slows"
on Ikorodu road
and close my eyes with the Jazz of
the bus with its interrupted radio sequence.

I will not join words with you
too many gallops
that make one fart in the pie-chart
 stuck at the mercy of the
laptop bag

Grant Me

My camera lens is getting shut gradually.
I lean on unstable waters of love.
When the thunder strikes
It'll wash me to the guts of my grave
I wish sometimes that my heart be made of stone.

I pray that my heart be made of stone,
 not tiny specks of dust
So my tears be dry and be without sound
And my anger without wrath
And my love without vaults.

I will lose much
But my loss will never be felt

The angel that prayed against this
Have not done well
They've made singers with questions
They made me seek Morenikeji with my life
And my tumult has grown from a rejection to a sore
cancer
Spreading to my ankle.

I pray for a heart of stone
Oh lord, grant me
That my words become a two-edged sword
That the warring wars of love should not capture me
in soothing shackles
Oh without a heart of veins and blood, I cannot
groan, I cannot whisper
I cannot tend my ears to the songs of a mirage
I cannot see the blooming flower and not notice the

fiery thorn
And the bitter smell
I cannot brood on words in my ARTery
I cannot dream of sex
Her wicked kindness cannot infect me.

Grant me-a heart of stone.

Go Slow

Put your soft trembling foam into your eyes
The silence of grumbling buses
In a long wait
Of passage
Muse in the earlobes
Amuse yourself with parading edible abuse.

Presage, peer and stretch your eyes
Into the marks, where yellow buses look like pints of
paint brush
Where the white UNILAG buses and the journey of
Abraham stage a coup

Go slow
Like protests barricaded by smoke
Even the walls feel their ghostly presence.

Go Slow
Simple ropes taut at uneven edges
By lorries of hurrying insanities

And UBA stands, empty, vomiting it's human contents
the banks close the markets
And the schools of young "no futures"
Throng out in the morn
Bouncing back
Like post cards in a chain of suspected expired drugs.

Poetry is non-sense
Poetry is scene-sense
Poetry is parameters of words
Pent-metre and words linked
Like long lines of multi-coloured vehicles.

Go slow
The destination is near
But pay homage to the God of potholes
That makes you shake like ping-pongs
That makes you jerk
Like after sequences of sex.

Nostos

I sing a certain song
When I speak to you
It's the tune that wakes me
Your name wells in me
But you aren't there to fetch it
To drink from my wine
And that
Is the way I know, I'm alone

The sun shines
And the crowd sprouts at the walkways
No butterflies in my garden ...
They talk in twos
I talk on a stage
No director's note,
No praise of prod
No anger
Just cold eyes
Holding onto the last warmth

I fear
Our story is not a miracle
Our story is not a revolution
Ours is a just a passing train
And passengers and passer-bys
Buy it
Without memories of its colour.

Heart Burns

White bread charred in earth's frying pan
The sensation of choking smoke
An accident of lovely truce
Leads to bush burning.

My heart warns me
Of the heat of love
The scorching unbearable loneliness
After the argument
The silence of newspapers
Loud in words but low on sounds.

My rival has your name stuck
On your tongue
His kiss is like 20 million stars
My crush is crushed
In the mud of strangulating caterpillars
Gnawing at my bones
Laughing at the gloves of my boxers.

My heart burns
And I wince.
My tongue folded like an unwanted blanket.
I look around
My glaciers melting
I have lost my cool

But I hold myself
And tell myself my foolishness

I now recite the hymn of melancholia
"To be lonely is no poetry
To be lonely is no laughter of characters
To be lonely is a shame- like touching yourself."

Greens take turns to the massacre
By fairies of fire
Yellowing outgrowths of my passion
Startled to its shocking death.
Birds of love songs relocate to
the uncomfortable abode of my intestines
The sun pretends that it is blind
To this genocide of my heart.

I look around
There is someone-
Just winds playing with dark dust
Like a child building castles in the air
The air is hard-stymied by fear...

I look around
There is someone
Just shattered porcelain
With crumbs of carbohydrate
The very last spared by locust.

The oil that burns my heart
Burns it well
My imagination soars like the sea
But damned in a dam...
Heart burns.

I need something to
 gather the shattered pieces
To sit still
And not steal glances
At my fears of impending doom.

Asiko

Asiko
Sneaking in on me
With a silent din
The illusions of memory
Flashing on aluminium plates

Asiko
My mind is a cybercafé
Sited are many thoughts
Processed with the preservatives of heat
The heat of patience booting in percentile

Asiko
Running without speed
For my hopes still linger
While my beards notify me-a weary landlord curse a
tenant with ten Naira
Who knows the termagant that nurtured this sperm?

Asiko
Births the wit
That whips up centenary sentiments
Asiko fancies my haircut
Dark turns to grey without the dye of style

Asiko
God's index finger
With a ring
That wrings us or wings us
Like the umbilical chord-
From which no man will live.

Poetry is my ever enduring lover

Fiction is my concubine
And the book is a bedspread
Drama is the noise that we make

Recantation

Death knocked
Barged in
Did not meet anyone at home

We came back
Called the carpenter
To fix the holds

That we may not be cold
Before the actual time
Unfold

Memories have a tendency to ripen

Or to turn bad
It's the natural order of things
They are fruit-things
That shade us from the scorching sun

Closed Shop

For Love is Marketing. Everyone is marketing something

D.E

Today,
I close my shop
I will no longer pay taxes
That tempt my eyes to a squinting
My goods are 'Not for Sale'
it is burnt beyond recognition
The market remains
Open
And the one legged, bow legged
deamons still come for a
Bargain
Speaking the silent language I no
Longer hear.

Today,
I close my shop
I can no longer wager the flood
That unearths the calabash of trade
'cantations
The screams of smiles and phone calls
The breather of blaring music
The chapters of banters and curses
I have left for the quietness of my closet
no more curse-stormers

I no longer
Aim to hit 'Jackpot'
I am no longer gambling with words
I am not frightened that
I have chosen a different path
Or lost my share of the stock-exchange
The world can scream for all I care
I have locked my shop

Why did the Chicken Cross the Road?
(For Benjamin Zephaniah)

Why did the chicken cross the road?
To form an alliance across the Niger
To join fellow chickens in a spree of cake
To become prominent-maybe, maybe not

Why did the chicken cross the road?
To campaign for vegetarian democracy, I guess
But chickens want to be rich and famous
Chickens want to preach
Chickens are brothers, sisters
Full of colour and prejudice

Why did the chicken cross the road?
To further its show-biz on a reality road show
you should ask the writer of the road
Chickens want libertine liberation
Chickens want social media pages, selfies-
chickens want to tweet at followers beck
Chickens want endorsements and awards
Want to crackle in British and American style

Chickens need to read
Contemplate
Chickens need to unite
And there will be no need to ask the question
Or to make chicken soup.

This House is 'Made in China'

This house is made in China
Our fears, that it does not lose its bricks
By the shifts of day

We wish that China be broken
So that our jetlagged friends keep coming
To buy us beer

We love Kunfu streaming on our faces
Buhda is the elite's vogue
But the China in our village tells a different tale

The frown of the colonial's face
Our lands for an expatriate
The kind of evil that happens twice

Our friends
Have become bloated by the sweat
On the migrant's back

The paperwork or the damp warehouse

Made in China
Translate in a manual to an African

Even China is made in China.

All my Forefathers

I.

I have forgotten the tales
the songs and the proverbs
and I am left with the seeming inspired adverts

I am or I was told
the reincarnate of the palm wine tapper
all I have tapped is the little oil in different taps
no more trees for tributes

I am the swimmer at the dancing braids of the lake
the favoured tadpole of the gods
alas, the waters have gone green with envy for land
the purity of sounds has left for the bubbles of fangs
nothing can swim,
except nylon, plastic and industrial spills.

I am the broken-hearted teacher
chewing textbook fantasies
galvanising theories at the detriment of truth

II.

My forefathers were warriors
dying in drowning truth bottles
migrating at the disgust of in-betweens

But at this behest of incest
we gather like insects to watch our denigration -
we have lost our will to fight
 we must lose our will to laugh

We have left the saving grace of a nation to politicians
we have cried to God but have forgotten who we are
and used to be
we have died the real death
And became living shadows.

We are foregrounded paintings of market activity
we are soap operas that take the review of all and
Oprah
we are newspaper columns without conscience
we are a people without leap, without patience

III.

I am no son of a slave
though trained with a slap
I need no bully as brother
I need no guerrilla as Government
I need no ruthless rut as redeemer
with nature, with sounds and with men
You all can see- all my forefathers lived in free and
fair contest.

Black

I have forgotten the forced hymnals of the forest
The strain of chain lockets
The banter of cracked teeth
The smile of anger and the heaves of harvest.

To be black
Is to be cautious
For I have been foresworn with a gun
Having none is betrayal of notion.

To be black
Is to be eternally wringed for wrongs
For I have been foresworn to be dumb
But not numb of passions' glow
Quick to blows! Brazen gold teeth, City holla caps
In the midst of Harlem hell.
Having none of these nose
Is a betrayal.

Hollywood
Cracks a hole in my heart
"Why are there no white street hustlers?
No white street-milling junkies?
It's all in the hood"
We ask for Cuban cigars or weed
While White is moved by coffee?
"make it black"-The White Police Chief
Why not "make it white"?

Black actors start to get white with fame
Move from Penn to estates at Newy
After the badge on the wall
They become ogres of whiteness.

I'm as black as black soap
That my forefathers bathed
By the Nile
Until Nihilism came
Along with the gentle temper of Christianity
Bold bodies, now shy in bathrooms.
Folded in wool
And swagger for dignity.

I'm just a temp
Watching my back for white folks everywhere
I'm just as black as I used to be
With Black Suits hung on the corridors of White
House...
This is America!
To be black is to be painted black
 If you're born black
You're 'pressed black
Like blackcurrants juiced with angry-sugar

This is America!
To be black is to be scribbled
"BLACK" on whiteboards of colleges
And yanked with a Police profile
"Black Male, Black Female"-(possible crimes of
blackness).

"You are black, can't you see!
You can run
Or ball and Funicate
You can blow and bruise
Or rap a tapping beat
And sing a snuggly song on death

You are black, can't you see!
We are neighbours
You have your mojo on-anytime!
Can't you see!

Techy

I'm a deacon with an Ipad of words; I also sow words on BlackBerry soil

My lady seeks to know with something called techno

My children greet me shouting WhatsApp
Must we families be linked with Linkedin or what is this world turning into?

I get requests everyday but I help by accepting, not giving.
I send requests and they retaliate-a world so unfair...
I use PIN to talk and gain response, yet it never pricks

No one sees well anymore, we all use Google

The next door neighbour is so lousy, when he starts to have fun with his wife, in heightened tempo "Yahoo, Yahoo!" is all that fills the lost serenity.

The sky has taken a hike, all that's left is Skype

I check my fridge to find something to eat and its all blogs; ah ah call the WordPress I want a press conference

Kudos to Steve Jobs, but here there's little or no jobs, so there's Jobberman

Books kind of lose space with Kindle, the tales leaves
you deep in the arms of Amazon
The worst that can happen in love is, talk to the hand,
report abuse, unfriend, without the pulse of blood
but with just a click

Love gains the signs of love, a smiling kissing
caricature, a lol for well-planned jokes
My wife pings a kiss every night and my son, tweets
me good morning. I don't beat him I poke him.

II.

The World is big enough
for Arabs
and Jews to
kiss without contact
For my fellow
country man
sextexting my wife
in the cold of the night

The world is big enough
to plunge into the sea
with Google maps and bad data
on your way to Ibadan

I have been tried by Americans
by blog posts
blog presence and opinion flirts
I feel the strain of being black here
without 'private' jets

The world is a class
big enough for a transsexual
classmate
a deeper living born Christian
And a Sheikh in front
the teacher is a skype form
no brawls can reach the eye
the projector doesn't shy

The world is a perception
mortar and pestle
can be mortar and mortar duels
I leave my rest to 'Big breasts and wide hips'

To Sleep

I'm on the cliff
Waiting for the wind
To take me across
Where no words can reach

I'm on the cliff
Weighing options
Laughing at my wounds
Singing
Without the treble of the heart

I'm on a cliff
Lost in a maze of thoughts
Hoping there's an easy way

To sleep and not wake

Listen

To the voice of the clouds
That streaming echo
Pregnant, swayed by the winds

Listen
to the bleating
Of goats
Satisfied with their fates
Anxious not of fraught natures

Listen
To temperate trees
Fondled by the wind
Firm in the sun
Housing the insects in their groin
Mending their wounds
By the silence of time

Listen
And try to forget about yourself
You are nothing
Your voice is a privilege lost on you
Your tact is prattle
You will never be calm
Your wounds will memorise the incident
You will be thankful for life
Unleavened
Unyielded to the winds

Beer Room Conversations

Response from a Chauvinist

I.

Manage your feminism
With fear and trembling
Because I paid your dowry
prostrated flat at the feet of your clan

You have your wind
Under my watchful eyes
For marriage started in the era of fiefdom
I am your god

The yams of my barn,
The fullest of goats
The boxes of clothes
Closed the chances for serial wealth

II.

Manage your feminism
With fear and trembling
Cook my food as at when due
And wrap your arms around my hungry force

I am not one of those
Weak men
Romantic drunks
Who say 'live and let live'

liberality has plundered the world
To be equal is to be independent
I don't want a divorce as well ...

III

We both have rights
But I am the referee
I decide when the ball
is over

Response from a Feminist

Leave the market women out of this
It is a matter for stories and theories
All men are equal but women are...

Mothers, daughters
Blisters of struggle
Men, modern serfs thrashing about
The grain of human backs

We make the most sacrifices
Our breast flaccid with the bite
Marks of babes
We cook and clean- the dream and the debris

We don't care about Elizabethan cosmopolitanism
We are ladies
To love and to hold

We are killing the male character
In our stories
All men are the same
Egoistical bastards

II

We are not afraid of single motherhood
With buoyant boys
 Ying is not restless without Yang

Mary is the mother of God

Allen Postcard

You are constipated of women
They are pudding to dip one's fingers
In the dark alleys

A yellow spot waving at cars
By its enhanced buttocks
Charging hopes on the weakness
Of a tired consumerist's libido

All I have for you
Bystander
Is respect

You will be remembered
For you have stretched yourself
To provide this service
Through your cervix.

A Pro is a Pro

A Prostitute is a Saint
That we castigate
Conerstone
Wet with knowledge
Of Demand and Supply
Hardworking generalismo

A Prostitute
Is a corporate strategist
The mystery packaged in dim
Shadows
Of few lights
Policeman. Eye to eye
Words like a prattleof a cat
Symphony sinks, the cold night whispers

A Pro is a Proust
A Superman
Reimagining our imaginations
Our envy of the pros
Comes from the chains that bind us
The chains we can never be free from
For truth thrives even in a great recession

A Pro is a Pro
A gift, a service delivered
Like Konga.com

For Beer Never Nags

Sweat and groan;
To my concubine, go I
The joy of friendship
Lasts in the mixture of known and unknown

She cools my heart
'my dear barley bottle'
She smiles and heart
Vanishes for warmth.

Fair and fat
Her sister who serves me
Beauty bleached best described
But never my concubine
Drawn from nature's spine
Spin into mine

For beer never nags

Her round lips wait
For my kiss and my words
Wants my tongue in her round hole
Patience that gladdens my heart
Laughter coursed my mouth

She's my saviour
My lover, as long as I want
When I don't have money she chills
Her full breast responds, gasp at every touch...

Her pregnancy never worries me
Still opens, a mall of my delight
'my dear ,never, your bikini hides nothing but your
hides open;
barley hides
For beer never nags

Discourse becomes disco or discuss
Headaches gone
Blues and fairy tales with mature
Tint.

She sits on my lap
Bearing her breast to my sensuous lips
To my tender touch without:
'WHEN, HOW, SHOULD YOU, WHY,
WHO, YEH, COME AND SEE,
WHERE, WERE YOU. WHAT HAPPENED'
For beer never nags.

Silence needs to repent
And bluntly spit that truth on my shirt
To stagger in a circling world
To press my thigh on her
Mutually groaning
She pops, I suck.

Whiteness!
Tomorrow is trouble again
Wife means Potiphar's wipe
Politics of a scheming type

Let my eyes be shut
From risky love
Let me be tired of touching
The one at home.

The frying pan bangs today
The new car is overheating
The cough originates from kitchen
The television has none of my vision
The cup is the shape of cunt
The heart is divorced while the rest distorts
The salary murdered at arrival
The attention is complained about
The sex is not hot like frying plantain
For beer never nags.

Gulder in my gall
Guinness raises the sperm in my penis
Satzenbraw lends me no brawl
Harp, sweet words, musical from harp
'Burukutu' drums the lyric of my fathers
'pleasant friend'
'Pleasant'
For beer never nags

Life is sweet with you my little 'punanny'
There are no family problems
After the daily dowry- CHEAP AS HELL
Nothing more
For Beer never nags.

The Journeyman

For Tope Mark

The journeyman
Once asked a question
About roadblocks
And makeshift bamboo sheds
Flouting the serenity of the shrubs

Men looked at him
Said he was a noisemaker
Men said he was a troublemaker

Said he was not born again

The Journeyman shouted hoarse
On many travels
One day he kept quiet for the sake
Of not being labelled a madman

The barricades has become demigods
They killed the men and raped the women

He walked without tyres

This Reincarnate Country

The country has lost her medicine
She drives her being into foreign thighs
Cocooned for respite

The country's sore legs
Sits like an amputee
The only knowing

Is the cackle of different tongues
and a Jihad march past
A hurricane of dust in the marketplace

This country
Is Robinson Crusoe's vast land
A wrestle for the control of the barn

Man-eaters in government
Palliatives in parliament
The sea distances the Isle of heaven

The country is an elephant
Dead-on-Arrival
Meat is shared on the outskirts of town

II.

The country births hope
when the marauder rides a fierce horse
She crawls

This reincarnate country
Is breathing fine
With a gas mask

And delightsome doses of experimental drug

Her pale skin glows
But she needs reconstruction
Man-eaters are learning edible leaves

The galloping horse broke its leg last week
It was told by transfers in a single account

This country
Baby steps
Photographs of unrestrained laughter

III.

The jihad is not over
But the voices are sunk in quicksand
We can find the clothing
Mementos of memory
Bathing near the Niger.

Good Night

One day
The world will fold
And birth a new layer of people
Pores of a new soul
All the noise of invention
We have made will be scrap

One day
The world will bend
Ans we will be ashamed
Of our stories
We will become 'exotic' finds
Of a once barbaric people

We tolerate the towering churches
Reminders of forced crusades
We mention the muse of mosques
Birthed by Jihads on animists
The legends are murderers of a whole lot

The new lords are the philistine tyrants
And we call it civilisation

And we bear civilisation well
With our mobile phones
From the sweat of unpaid Japanese
We bear civilisation well
From the cut and dried lies of art criticism
We bear civilisation well

From cartoons, stereotypical cartoons
Of George of the Jungle, Alaadin and the Fourty
Thieves
And the picture of Jesus as white as snow,
As white as Lord Lugard,
As white as lies
It is lies that make the world go round.

No One will remember You

With your writer's fellowships.
It will leave your name
Greying out like greens in the season of drought.

No one will worship at your facebook profile
Unless you remind them,
It will not be firm
It will not be one, two, three, like Christopher Okigbo

No one will read you
Except writers like you
Your language is the tone of the rich
Your mood conspires with your pretence
Your face does not ring a bell except,
On Chimurenga, Saraba, Sankofa, Granta,
Anything the mould of writers looking for
Grants

The man next door does wonders
What you do for a living?

No one will share your life
You're too upside down
Flown here and there with passion
And drowning with none
Your smile is signature soothing

Your anger will burn the entire dynasty of thoughts

Your life is lonely
So you party hard to make an impression
With your impasto flaunts
Like the fishwife –
Stale stench of phlegm from children,
The rite of fish and the browning water
The dirty talk of breasts
Sudden fuck like pump action.

In the end
It will fall to nought
Recycled over and over again
By rebel universities
And hardly successful pitchforks.

In the end
It will be a ghost town
Blown away by the triumph of dust
Shared on a crumbling wall.

Image

It is beautiful to be like God
the Spectral Guardian
With no antecedent

Postcards for Irene

Ex Lovers

The Slant scribble is a signature of scars
the Freudian muse of mounting memories
cheques bounced at the counter

Ex-lovers are like schools
For bourgeoning expatriates
They change the pictures of your brain
For value is a matter of impression

Ex-lovers can be complicated
Dry ink can rise again
Pump price can soar again
You can become the big fish in the Times
Old things shall pass as art
And new things can become fart.

Twin Children

For Dignified

Writing is the first wife
It gives birth to twins every night
And they cry
There wails come in stanzas

I cuddle them in my arms
and feed them on tablets
I sing them a lullaby
But they refuse to
Sleep

They add a chorus to my song
A symphony that wakes the neighbours
To the quiet noise
I hand them over to their godmothers
Huge Cherubims
With wings like doves
Wings the size of love

And they fall asleep

Leaving me awake
Dejected
Cold
Without a woman by my side

Gbemisola

Gbemisola
When you lift me to your chest
I feel
Walnuts of memories

I can feel you
The very you behind the bra
And behind the denim

I can feel you
the signature belly button
gnawing at my sides
and your laughter
that honeyed chirping
of a humming bird
that nectared bossom
that blossoms.

I am a lone bottle now
Floating in the lagoon
like a lost bottle down the Ganges

I am alone now
Wide awake on concrete pillows.

*Performed alongside the Amororo Music Dynasty, a juju band based in I
badan at the African Court Night*

The Circle of Days

I.

You make me melt
Like hot chocolate
And hard like cake
I crumble
In your tender lips

I die a pleasant death
When I dip my finger in your
Tender pudding

I gush
Like a river from the rock
It cleanses my mind of worries
When we stream into one
The miracle of water tasting like Juice

I am immune from frostbite
My heat comes from the sun
And from the clothing of naked truth

I am awake to the first splash of sunlight on the river
bed
Warm memories that greens the leaves
And yellows the fruits

I love the circle of the day
That births the circle of the night
The river never sleeps

I am long music for the idle fisherman
And calm for the burnfires of the midnight

The fishes fiddle around the underbed
Whispers and lucid conversations
Rocks from molecules cake into picturesque statues

II
I am a dirty
Lonely pond without you
For tortoise and snails

The wings of banana leaves
Foreshadows the sun

I cannot stream
the soul does not burn

I smell the death of life
murdered by the flood

With rays of hope
Eclipsed by the shell of another planet

My hands cannot peel
The blanket of boredom

For tortoise speaks in monotones
And snail with leaves in their sacred mouths

The snail is a sage taking its time to mourn the sun
The tortoise is learning the act of aloneness

When will clouds surrender to the sun
And birth a river from the rocks?

I long for volcanic dispatch
After a lonely meal of mush

I long for flowers in the hair of stems.

Getting High in Sleep

I have dreams of you
the brief lull from insomnia
I drown in your smile

Your memorable laughter
Your dimpled face
Your supple skin

I travel to your embrace
But you tease me with a peck
You ruffle the hair on my chin
And make a joke

There is nothing without you
In the room of my head
The dawn that lights my hightower

You are the sparkle that lights my torch
The crevice of my being culls you
Beside me, you blossom everyday.

Old Together

I am an angry, bad mouth felon
But she loves me
She is a rusted anchor of complaints
But I love her, more than I love anything

I am the late comer and the slight eater
As if the soup is not sweet
She is the one who refuses me on that lofty place
But I love her and she loves me.

I am the ruffian, fussing here and there for things not
missing
She is the silence when silence is the need
I am the butt of her jokes when the fuss is over
When lost is found and scattered becomes arranged.
I love her though I do not tell her, she knows
She loves me though she is too old to call me stupid
names like 'darling'

Our album is full as our cups are
Our children have gone away and we are children
again
Longing for companionship not as rough as it began

It will soon be over
How soon we do not know
But it will be that of full smiles of old honeymoon
Transcending in a compass of time
We are old, old together

Longlisted for the BN Poetry Prize 2015

The Plosive of Love

To love you
Is to make my heart transparent
To become fluid in your arms of trust
To forget and remember...

To love you
I can sing the songs of troubadours
Long, lengthy and tiring
Energized by the wine of your smile
You have bought me over
your platinum sympathy
By your laughter

You are my music
Unstopped by the shadows of past doubt
You are my cool evening breeze
With the sky, a canvass of an artist's hand

You are my nightfall
Of tender moments turned dreams
Dreams of childhood memories
Dreams of 'Aladdin
Dreams of heaven- me, you and the praise of the
cherubim

You are my nightfall

A poem is not enough
It is a tribute of a tributary
It is but a din of sound in an opera
It is an utterance plosive
Yet to explode

New-Inverse

The Class Act

I have broken up with Poetry
Now gay with QWERTY
I make them lab rats
They do not pay the bills

All writers must come out of space
To see without the translucent foil of living it

The class act of performance
We are more, amore
We are dour, adore
We are core, hardcore

We are dead-lines listening to the muse
But doing more with disuse

We are drunk on ourselves
a tableau above the peer review

Nothing sacred
Living it, loving it, drowning in it
Like a drunk bastard without a day's job

We are lost in the labyrinthine walkways
Holding hands but going nowhere
Only few will find their way to engraved tombs
Markers of a massacre

Ours is a death with a shout
Strained to hear it ourselves.

A View of the City from a Pressed Bed

Beside me is a menstrual flow
Of emptiness
Gathering aside a numbness
Of passion
Shaken by the sequences that may coalesce
into nothing

My room faints
Into incoherence
Like war radio from a secret station
That pitches the proud against the pained
Bombs drop pound for pound into the village of hope

The castle is built of uncertainties
Where violence fixates upon residues
Of repetition
Where the weak is buffeted by
Strongholds of mercantilist bribe
And the strong bully of diplomacy

The niceties of war are now in the
Supermarts
Displayed by populist consumption
Of values

Pain is the bread of life
Stirring a blurry satire
An undiscovered landscape of things
Bones of dinosaurs
Under centuries of brick

Pain is the latitude
Of the sea
Where migrant blood stirs
And homeland blood stares
Hoping to be brushed by the hip with ecstasy
To be validated by the motions of history
In post-textual conversations
Pain is searing like sickle cell anaemia

What flows tonight is petrol
It gives a flush on one's black face
From the grief of limitation

What hums tonight is fear
Freezing
The oils of bonfires
The interstice of the cities without lights
With an aloofness to graphic delights
 But with a script that replays itself

The tourist keeps up
With the first impressions
Honeymoon music
That shatters
Into glib notes of
Survival sonata
The crisis of the age is realism
Satre, Fanon, Bhaba, Montesquieu

Sleep beckons a weakness
Wakefulness
Pricks with reflection
Nothing goes unpublished
From the memory of tombstones.

Q

First you take their names off
And they become a cricket
Hiding in the corner of your room

Then you cut the wings
Of the memories you have with them
And they become a blurred shadow
A lost scroll , lost to the fire
Misen-scene

Mankind will leave you
Cold in the sun
Burnt in the shower
And strapped on a bed

The Poet Died

The poet died
In those who look for money
And cheat fellow poets of their means
she will not be saved by an asylum
nor festivals, no impresario bandying

The poet died
In a clogged room like a tax collector
Playing god
Poetry is not a wrestling match
Mud fights are for idiots

The poet died
When the metaphor is too beautiful
But the carpetbagger's praise prods on

You want to become primma donna
You want a laureate from your dreams
You flick a cigar like a profiler and turn with attires

You are not a poem
She is at the drawing board garnering dust.

On the outside walls
I am a gladiator
With scars to show
Mementos of greatness
Accompanied by songs

The best hands have been engraved
In a mass mould of songs

Which refer to my sword
That silvery flash that brings me pain
That blacksmith curse that has torn my heart
From my flesh

The survivor is wreaked
Weakened by memories
Of lost things
Stifled by impotence
Crippled by urgencies of time

Unloved by the changing weather

I long for a conversation with the dead
To recall nostalgia
That lacks guilt and pain
Or a blunt picture of blood
Cascading down my veins

I long for warm presences of truth
The living is filled with deceit
Competing for green grass
the living wants words that woo, that soothes
that panders
words that leave the truth in the throes of death

I am travelling in the loneliness
That greatness knows
Hard ground is the only route to high ground
Paid is the only way to resurrection
Blood is the only choice for propitiation

A Shot of Muse

My poet
That smokes Indian hemp
That delves into origins
With his tooth
That sings after every shot
of muse
My poet
An addict of salt
A luminary of a carton of beer
The man booker of bukas

The Scholar of scholaris
Child of the Portuguese, British and Bambara
Burnt black Nigerian
With stomach churning

Self-exile with travel
Naked before the sea
Waiting for the total force
Of the Nigerian plague.

The Nod

There are no elders here
Only old people

Dereck Walcot

They want to suck me
my blood is sweet
It was brewed in the ancestral groove
where trees fellowshipped with the history
of clay
discovers itself by quietude

They want to wrap their tongue around
my head
and drain me
they claim 'it's service'
an American double-speak for enslavement
it is an 80/20 Principle where wealth/loss handshakes

I am the laughter
that knows you want to cheat me
my heart let it go
hunger must last for a while

I come from a place
where laws are broken by an older face
where fresh is granted as taken
where my blood is sweet white like new wine

but time will come
when I will take it no more
I will shake all your hold
and let your crippled legs fall
I will yank your stick from you
and kill you will silence
when you scream for help

—----

A sojourner once sang
'It is the forerunner that shows
the way in a dark place'
It is the song of lore that keeps
You along the route
where water pools in the land of drought

But yours is a race full of malicious, raucous
maraduers
with bagfuls of the greed of blood
your race is Achitophel
renewing itself with wars of pain
your race surrounds a story of betrayal
gawping at downfall that meets your knees.

I forgive you
I travel in the knowing of a lone traveller
my journey meets rare guides amongst tricksters
my way is not new but my stride is
I weigh the doctrine of a few

but carve a new religion for myself

I am the renegade that knows
how to wield a sword
how to laugh in a meal and a drink
with my enemies
pain teaches never to be drunk in love

I see your struggle
the greyness of your stride
and I feel for you

I will soon get to where you are
but blood will never be my meal

I wrap my face with silence
and give a nod when paths meet
you have been here before me.

Stone Upon Stone

I

When I think of stone
I do not sing like African poets
With metaphors of fetishes
I do not look upon stone as an ebony continent
I do feel stone as mystic walls

When I think of stone
I recount the god of poetry
Whose verse took the jewish act
And turned pent-coastal
With the memoir that stone wrote

When I think of stone
I do not prophesy a stone as Peter
Whose name patters out with Paul's oratory
I think of Julius Berger and Julius Nyerere
Jutus Julius

II

When I think of stone
I see the early fire of survival
Hunger and loneliness
Wrestling with the animal
And making warmth
Flesh upon bone

When I think of stone
I hear the song of hunters

Sharpen their knives and spears
For hunt
Praising Ogun
And reserving faith in a gourd of palmwine

I think of boulders that pre-exist
Where ancestors rested their backs
A place yet to be seen
There lay altars of first coming
Output of the strong and refuge for the weak
Omniscience without the deceit of a greying
moustache
In the guise of godliness

III

When I think of stone
glint of pearls on the lace
clothing my grandmother
sold at a bargain for mother's textbook
faith in a child's treasury

When I think of stone
I notice the grindstone
The leg scrubber
The door stopper
The rock of ages where oil drips in prayers

IV

When I think of stone
I taste the pebbles of tablets
The tongue is the palm of life and death

When I think of stone
I swallow in the anguish
of daily trance
weighed by motion without movement
Lavender without Love
Grace without Gracias

When I think of stone
I traverse Ikoyi pavements
Rocks upon vaults of history
a city dies
Rebirths like phoenix
With the birthmarks of colonial names

When I think of stone
I think of traffic
bleaching the black
Going to the German bundesliga
that relegates you to a sofa
of failed gladiators

When I think of stone
I see graveyard in marble
Shutterstocked in the memory of loved ones
Like vaults in the manoselum
The work of grinding is over for some

When I think of stone
I think of missing things
Missing hearts, missing appendices, missing you
Memories that make me gasp for breath
And restrain my tears.

V

I think of David Livingstone
From one corner
A slingshot identity of an other

When I think of Stone
I reflect upon terbanacles and podiums
The kind that manacles your difference
To a chair
Power to St. Francis

When I think of stone
My heart praise God
Only two stones hold the world together

My sweat

Is my blood
It drops as I rail through my path
An earphone of escape
A pocket of temperament
A life that is not a life
Of dreams

Long Walks

I don't believe in love
But i give myself to people
Draining blood from a bite of my vein
I die a dozen times
To bring relief ...

I never find fresh air
In the promised serendipity of prophets

I will myself
To shutdown from an
Umbrage stroking my door
Gnawing at my back

I want to elope with myself
To a place where I can make sense of it all

There is no point living
In utter pain
Better pray for death
The quicker the good

I put up a smile
By my eyes gives away the status
I walk long walks
Bungling myself against the dust

Walks are my own weeping
Walks are my placebo to madness
Walks are my illusion to progress
I walk a dozen times

Next week, I will walk again
Transcend to a postcard in your frame
A temporary voice
You will never remember my name.

Pastiche

Soliciting for stage
In an underground garage
For friends who had once
Done it
Are tired

Life conscripts you
Into a suitcase
Makes a poem your career
And turns people against you

Drop your fucking 'Tobi'
For hyphenated dreams
Like crisp ten naira notes
In the hands of beggars

A poet with smooth words
Confident
With dark poetry
In the midst of starry eyed newts

A fog in the room is repetition
A failed motif
A strangled metaphor
Every poem is searching for the ideal

A Painting is not a tattoo
A painting is Egon Schiele, Mozart,
Soyinka in a transfiguration with a fourth.

No punch lines in heaven
For those who have crossed the sea.

In a Gallery of a Geisa

For Charles Bukowski

You sit in a bar
Listening to the lowered din
of a popular song
the party is over and the giggles echo
through your veins

There was a time when that same bar
Was thriving with your ego
Your happiness smeared the wine cup
With a certainty of drunken love

Women
Cerebrospinal metasis
That flow into your core
And make you lost for words

Women
Muse and music
The milk shakes of bellicose verse
Floundering words of spontaneous poetry

You slam yourself on the bed
Your eyes scan through the room
The warm things in your room
Are cockroaches mating and minding
Their meals

The debris of the mind
Longs for a tender soaking, foaming,
Shower, towelling
You sleep in the unkempt

Sleep takes you to a place where sense is illusion

A woman teases you with illumination
That sends electric charges to your armoured tank

There are no world wars to wage
You wake up hugging the pillow
Multi-functioning
Your eyes are bloodshot from the terror of the night

Women
Subtle smile, fiery anger
Strutting with high-heeled authority
Glowering in their frame
Urgeing you to champion
A jihad for their souls.

You cannot touch the archived photo
You see the ringed arm has a depth of mundane
semiotics
You marvel at the pictures of hairdo, and hair down
in the underground alleys.
You pretend that your mind is satisfied by work alone.

Work down the dark is the only splendid work
The gallery closes by 5pm
The officialise turns a tongue
But no one heads to your part of the city
You slum, your silhouetted chasm

The traffic kills you
Because some unknown brushes her
Backside on your navel
There are times when you marvel at how
Everyone wants to get home

Mannequin

A fair lady with a cracked medulla
Another with a broken arm
Bandaged by cellotape

He wears a hat
Holds his shoes
Scared of the market of threats

She is naked
Full with plastic desire
With her see-through panties

They are hung on the balcony
Like sex workers
with loud music

What if she has got STDs
From the dust of the road
Or the putrid gutter
Thick as African Soup

She carries a fashionable bag
Half as big as Ghana Must Go
She stays in the heat
Waiting for customers
Like you.

Bathrooms

All great poets are looking for new metaphors
Not washed-out wrappers of last year's new yam festival

Coldplay with warm water
Splashes
Soap suds on my Sambisa forest
And my artillery

Bathing is like motorcycle maintenance
Classical movements
Seeming art
Without another eye

Thoughts bounce
In this archaeological room
Where the debris of our lives
Are memories without database

We cake at the tiles

The bathroom is a studio
Self record without the cloud of judgement
Dance that watches his steps

The ritual that never counts
The balm of chemical lustre brushed against your
nipples
An ablution that signals a fresh day

The sanctuary of resolutions
To mark time with bodily changes
To have pulsating sex there
To waste less water.

Two Legs

This is a Voice

The Music of my voice
Is bold
Yet it does not sing
It does not announce itself

The music of my voice
Is a rushing train
With Russian tenacity
It does not wait for the comprehension
Of colours

The music of my voice
Is not soothing
Not all the time
It is cruising the potholes
And crashing at the vegetation
Near the sidewalks

The music of my voice
Has a voice vote
In a cabinet of knives
Forks and spoons
The poison can still be rendered
In 3D motion picture

The music of my voice
Is alternative Fuji
Or Soft rock—I don't know
Reggae without dreads
Drawls of Country
Highlife or hybrid confusion.

Why we do These Things

We do these things
To justify ourselves
To kill the sisiphyian
With memories of created progress

We do these things
To count our days
To fund sleep through exhaustive means
If times were better
We wouldn't

We wish that better times
Will gush from the pipes
And our thirst will not be lost on it

What else can we do
With so much passion, angst and love

It is not good
to mark the sands of time
Like Chicken running from an eagle

II

The world does not need another
Sacrifice
On the crossroads
It has gobbled too much
With its saliva of rain
The World does not need
Tears and handkerchiefs

The World does not need
Saviours

It wants gladiators, powerful princes
It yearns for make-believe
It sighs at controlled chaos

If the world is filled
With drug addicts
We should be the peddlers
If the world be a cage
We should have a spare key
To tranquillity

For change is a fashion copy
And love
Is for Christmas and Valentine
The world is not art
We should not be its rags

The world needs no sacrifice
On the crossroads
It has been hasty
Flooding scapes with mouth-watering
Feast on promissory sun.

Dakar

For Tade Ipadeola

Senghor's place
Mother sun shines on the throne
Of a settled herdsman

Dakar woman
Whose skin
Dulls my pain
Song from the clacking of empty gourds
Drunk by my stomach god
Have you found the dream
Of Nilowe
Or is it just a dean of dreams
A franklin on a grassland?

Have you found the dream
Of papa
Has the sunset drowned your dreams?
Wake up
The music of the birds
Will bring the sun in bits
Let your voice never be scuffled
No more French silence

Eye
(for Niyi Osundare)

God is reading the Washington Post
Bidding the angels to reduce the noise
Of their praise
Fine grains of men chant Ahaili* in the desert
And God drops his paper

God is dancing to men's drums
As they clap from the sand dunes
Poets are the strings that hold God's heart

For God floats in their skies
And lightning up their minds to words

But do not mistake God for shivering flowers
Or soaring seas
Do not say you have seen Him in rocks
God sits near the musing of poets
The all seeing eye
Without a telescope.

Performed at the 2015 Niyi Osundare Poetry Festival at the University of I badan.

The Congress of Memory

for Niyi Osundare

Before me is a ladder of words
before my naked astral
as I wrestle with words
for a congress

that spread from here to elsewhere

My destiny is a tranquil journey
clear as the obstacles beckon
for prophets have gone before me
Post-colonial hymnals

Post-post colonial protests
folklore and imagery nuanced
by the signature of my tongue

I face myself
in a telephone conversation of grey hairs
but I see youth
in a playground of growing milk teeth

Before me
is a reincarnation of bards
Hunters and priests, eulogers and patricians
Enslaved by the chaos of chains or chalices

Gropping in the dark for the light of a voice.

Poetry is not child's play
But it is from a child's play
Those elders know where a child's path leads

I am a Hightower
earning the praise of every sail
giving thanks to the gifts of the ancestors
every gear of a new voyage

Is a subtle plagiarism
every verse is a modern proverb

There are 'more mouths to feed'
More songs to yarn
More journeys to tale
Before I join the congress of Memory.

A Biographical Note
For Iye Osundare

A child is born
A child whose screams
Becomes a national song

His mother
A noble priestess of marketplaces

A child is nursed
On the herbs of Osun
A river traversing the rocks, the barks of trees
And the earthly pots

His mother a traveler
Barefoot with her wares
Upon the hilly landscape

A child becomes a poet
From the cannon fodder of mother's philosophy
His mother becomes the Selah
Of the age's composition

A mother is a bulb
Encyclopedic streams of dreams
That builds the poet's cantos
From his mother's ourve.

A poet is a stayer
In his pouch is nostalgia
Of his landscape
The victories of love
That culls a metaphor into songs

95

Mothers are syncretic beings
They worship their sons with Oriki
Sculpting their heads at every bath
leaving behind seven white birds hovering over their
heads.

A River's Child

Water rebels against the hegemony
of the edge
She groans in an apartment with a lonely
Song

Water claims its land
from the conquest of man
for no truce was made
and the elements of hate festered

Water protested
a plosive after a long-suffering
surging from the banks
to the banks of earthly treasures

Water waged a battle
without a rainbow flag in sight
without the esigna of the star spangled banner

Katrina tramples on its friends
blinded by the surge to punish

Orleans woke Osun in its sleep

Katrina vexed
but forgot that a river child
Never dies from water

Katrina quotes Elliot
And Osun sways to a proverb of songs

Katrina flips the pages
Over-reaches like a militant

But a river child cannot choke
By a body of water
A river child cannot float
Lifeless from the river of elsewhere

Katrina immortalizes itself
With scrawls of dilapidation
Katrina collects the treasure of tears
Katrina forgets the element of memory.

Author's Note

To my parents, my personal Orishas, whose love and endurance is a living autobiography. One of my great fears is to find myself unable to acknowledge and reciprocate your love and service to me before your passage to the ancestral scape.

To Aramide, fore-sojourner, I remember the laughter as you tease great writing out of me, as you prod me with praises for work undone. Your passing keeps me bleeding every day.

I am grateful to my brothers, Enoch and Bunmi, and other brotherhoods; The Baron's Café. I am aware of the bond of mighty men, Ademola Adesola, Olalade Adewuyi, Tokunbo Dada, Segun Ayoade, Oyin Olofinlua, Innocent Ekejiuba,Trust Obe, Nwilo Bura Bari, Oluwasogo Faloye and the Favourite Son of Africa.

To Tade Ipadeola, poet laureate, I am grateful for so many things. To Silva Imal, Sir Adewumi Adedeji, 'Dotun Eyinade, Jahman Anikulapo, the CORA Team, Dr. Senayon Olaoluwa and Dr. Sola Olorunyomi, you have all made a rebel shine.

The women in my life have been good to me, Jane, Ope, Fiyin, 'Yomi, Febi, Tobi, Nne, Anthonia, Adeola and the list goes on. To Unoma Azuah, Anwuli Ojogwu, Azafi Omoluabi-Ogosi, Temitayo Olofinlua, Lilian Shoroye and Jumoke Verissimo, thank you.

To Poet Laurete, Tanure Ojaide, Adebiyi Olusolape, Neils Hav, Stephanie Shonekan, for the encouragement that are the back stories that make life meaningful.

To Jumoke Lawal, Busayo Togun and Dupe Kuku who urge me to hold on to poetry even if it is a gift that earns neither reputation nor funds.

Wale, Sidi, Rasheed, Ifeh and REZ, thank you for trust.

Femi Morgan
Ibadan
(2012-2018)

ABOUT THE AUTHOR

'Femi 'fairchild Morgan is a writer, entrepreneur and creative and public relations executive. He is the author of chapbook, Silent Drummings (2008), co-author of the Sankofa Chapbook, Phases: Poetry of People (eds 2015) and Songs of Travel, Artmosphere Nigeria Chapbook (2016). 'Femi Morgan is the co-recipient of the 234Next Fashion Copy Prize. He was long-listed for the BN Poetry Prize in 2015 and was selected for the Writvism Writing Workshop in 2015.

His literary works have been published on several media like Eureka, Jalada, African Writer,Saraba, Sentinel Nigeria, Praxis Magazine, Happenings.com, Fortunate Travellers, The Guardian and others. He has performed his works at the Lagos Book and Arts Festival, African Court Night at the Institute of African Studies, Laipo Reads at the American Corner, Alliance Francaise and others.

'Femi Morgan is the curator of Artmosphere, a leading culture, arts, and conversation event which has been held in Nigeria for seven years. He has been host to numerous creatives, intellectuals, philosophers and bards such as Niyi Osundare, Tanure Ojaide, Sam Omatseye, Ros Orlando Martins, Jumoke Verissimo, Victor Ehikhamenor, Beautiful Nubia, Chuma Nwokolo, Ayo-Ola Mabiaku, Niran Okewole, Tade Ipadeola,Tunde Adegbola, Remi Raji, Ahmed Maiwada, Micheal Afenfia, Amu Nnadi and others.

Femi Morgan is also an investor and entrepreneur in the culture scene with interests in media, content development, public relations, culture events curation and management. He has been media content editor, and contributor at thisisafrica.me, dstv.com, afrima.com, and Quramo.com.

He lives in Lagos, Nigeria.

    fairchild09

Writer, Culture Curator and PR Executive
httpp://fairchildmedia.com.ng

Printed in the United States
by Baker & Taylor Publisher Services